BYGONE NORTHAMPTON

———————————

The Market Square has been a centre of trade since time immemorial.
A small knot of customers gathers round a secondhand stall in about 1910.

BYGONE
NORTHAMPTON

Alan Burman

Phillimore

1996

Published by
PHILLIMORE & CO. LTD.
Shopwyke Manor Barn, Chichester, West Sussex

ISBN 1 86077 021 5

Printed and bound in Great Britain by
BIDDLES LTD.
Guildford, Surrey

List of Illustrations

Frontispiece: The Market Square, *c*.1910

The Second World War

Acknowledgements

All of the photographs reproduced in this book are from the author's collection, gathered together over forty years, thanks to the generosity of fellow Northamptonians who have either donated pictures or allowed me to copy images in their possession.

In most cases the original photographers are unknown, but I owe them a great debt of gratitude. The results of their craftsmanship were treasured in their day, and thereby survived the years to be even more precious now.

I am indebted to Mr. Cyril Arnold, a long-serving press photographer, who took many of the wartime pictures and some of the 1930s.

The staff of the Northampton Central Library, particularly those of the local study room, have been extremely helpful, looking up long forgotten incidents and dates with unfailing good humour and patience.

Finally, my thanks go to all of those local folk who, over the years, have written to me or taken me aside after one of my slide shows, to tell me anecdotes from Northampton's past, to point me in the direction of some little-known facet of local history, or to add a snippet more to my knowledge.

If, despite all this assistance, there are any errors and omissions in this volume they are mine and mine alone.

Introduction

This is unashamedly a photographic dip into Northampton's recent past, not a comprehensive history of the town.

The first practical photographic process, capable of 'drawing with light', was announced in 1839. The century and a half that has followed is a mere eye's blink in the lifetime of Northampton. Yet, in that short time, there have been vastly more pictures created than in the many centuries before. Pictorially, it is the best recorded period of history ever. Such has been the influence of the camera.

Curiously, the basic elements of photography had been known for many centuries. Cameras had been used by Chinese scholars in ancient times and had spread until the principles were well recorded outside China by A.D. 1000. The phenomenon of light sensitivity must have been apparent equally early, not least upon ripening fruit. The first documented demonstration of the action of light on silver-based chemicals was by Johann Schulze in 1725. The problem was how to fix the image. Swedish chemist Carl Scheele separated exposed from unexposed liquid chemicals with ammonia in the 18th century. This was the first efficient fixer, although Scheele did not realise its significance.

Now, what has all of this to do with this book, you are asking? Well, had all of these separate discoveries come together we should have had photographs at least a hundred years earlier. The Jacobite Rebellion, the swearing-in of Washington, the French Revolution and the Battle of Waterloo would have been captured by camera. On a local level just imagine what this book would have been like!

No one knows just how old Northampton is. Ancient tribes must have occupied the site, for it was a fine defensive position, on a south-facing eminence protected on two sides by the river. Fresh water was there in abundance from many springs, springs so pure that they were the basis of a thriving brewing industry in later years.

The origin of Northampton's name is open to at least two theories. In the Saxon Chronicles it is written as Hamtune, an appellation adopted by several local businesses and currently the favoured choice. Others aver that the name derives from the river called by the Romans the Antona. Domesday Book therefore refers to the town as Northantone.

As the Roman empire declined and disintegrated and the garrisons withdrew from England, the country was infested with marauding bands, first Danes and then Saxons from North Germany. In 1010 the town was plundered and razed to the ground by the Danish king Sweyn and his army.

William the Conqueror brought stability by subjugating the warring factions, but he had no easy time of it. One of his fiercest opponents was Waltheof. Diplomatically, William recognised the leadership qualities of his defeated foe, made Waltheof Earl of Northampton and, in 1070, arranged his marriage to Judith, the Conqueror's niece. Judith, however, plotted her husband's downfall and falsely accused him of supporting the baron's revolt. Waltheof was executed at Winchester in 1076.

In William's entourage was a brave Norman knight who had fought alongside the Conqueror during the invasion of England. The name of Simon de Senlis crops up in many aspects of Northampton's history, usually as a benefactor, but it might have been very different. Upon Waltheof's death William proposed Senlis as Judith's second husband. Senlis was lame in one leg, perhaps as the result of a wound, and the cruel Judith rejected the match, refusing to marry the 'cripple', much to Senlis's relief. He immediately married Judith's daughter, Maud, thus inheriting the late Waltheof's rich estates.

Simon de Senlis supported the Priory of St Andrew, in the northern section of the town, with great generosity. He granted All Saints' Church, nine other religious establishments, many houses, much land and considerable income to the priory. He also repaired the decaying abbey buildings.

But the most spectacular work of this Norman knight, a veteran of the first crusade, was the construction of Northampton Castle and the town's defensive walls, in about 1084. The walls were formidable, the top forming a road wide enough for six people to walk abreast. Four main gates allowed access: the South Gate adjoined the river bridge on the road to London with a chapel dedicated to St Thomas of Canterbury and St Leonard's leper hospital nearby, the North Gate where Regent Square is today, the West Gate near West Bridge, and the East Gate close by today's Abington Square. A fifth, and smaller, gate led to the river and the cow meadows and was known as the 'dierne gate', Old English for 'secret gate'. This thoroughfare is today called Derngate. The town at this time, according to Domesday Book, had 295 houses occupied and 35 empty or derelict.

Henry I was entertained at the castle in 1106, comfortably, one assumes, for he returned in 1123 with his court to celebrate Easter here in lavish style. Eight years later he again came to the castle to convene parliament. At this meeting the squabbling English barons were obliged to swear loyalty to Maud, the king's daughter, upon whom he had settled the right of succession. This royal favour seems to have brought prosperity to the town, for it expanded rapidly at this time.

1164 is a key date in Northampton's history; it is the date of the most famous incident in the town's past—the trial of Thomas à Becket. In defiance of Henry II's statute that ecclesiastics offending against the laws of the land should be tried by civil courts and not the church, Becket was summoned to Northampton Castle to answer charges of perjury and contempt. He was lodged at the Priory of St Andrew during the trial and went forth to meet the king dressed in full pontifical regalia of cope and mitre and bearing a silver archiepiscopal cross aloft. This infuriated the king who stormed off, sending back, via a messenger, his sentence. Becket, refusing to recognise the king's authority, returned to the priory from where, under cover of night, he escaped to France. After six years of exile, punctuated by political manoeuvring and intrigue, Becket returned to England and his death at the hands of murderers in Canterbury Cathedral just after Christmas in 1170. The well on the Bedford Road without the 'dierne gate', where Becket had refreshed himself as he escaped the king's sentence, was rebuilt by the corporation and covered with a fine stone canopy in 1843.

Henry II honoured Northampton by granting its first charter in 1185. This was reinforced by a second charter issued by Richard I upon his accession, which placed Northampton on an equal standing with London and allowed its citizens all the free customs and liberties enjoyed in the capital.

Royal favour continued under the next sovereign, King John, who visited the town on no less than 31 occasions. Northampton's staple trade of shoemaking was well established by this time, for the king bought a special pair of boots in the town in 1213 for which he paid the princely sum of 9d.

The town was rapidly becoming a centre of learning. Scholars of Oxford and Cambridge, universities plagued by students' riotous behaviour, came to Northampton. In 1258 a university was started with the king's blessing but when the students became embroiled in the de Montfort rebellion supporting the insurgent barons, tutors at nearby Oxford, with their livelihoods threatened, persuaded the king to abolish the Northampton establishment and banish the students. To this day Northampton has no university, although modern-day moves are afoot to upgrade Nene College to this status.

There were at least five orders of monks established in the town in medieval times, many of whom were entertained by King Edward I when he visited in August 1290. When his queen Eleanor died at Harby in Leicestershire later that year these same monks watched over her body as it passed through, and briefly rested, in Northampton on its way to London. In memory of this the king commanded a fine cross to be erected on the hill at Hardingstone overlooking the town, a monument which still survives.

More parliaments were held at the castle. In 1328 Edward III's parliament concluded a peace with the Scots which effectively gave them autonomy. He convened another parliament there in 1338 although he was away in France and was represented by the Black Prince. The fourth and last parliament to be held in Northampton took place in 1381 under Richard II. It was at this meeting that poll tax was first introduced at the rate of three groats per head upon all persons above the age of 15 and led to the rebellion of Wat Tyler and Jack Straw. These four parliaments are vividly pictured carved in stone around the steps of the present Town Hall.

Henry VI, who followed, is recognised for having given Northampton its first charter of incorporation and establishing the title of mayor in 1445.

In the main the Wars of the Roses, which washed over the country soon afterwards, left Northampton relatively undisturbed. A notable exception was the Battle of Northampton which occurred in July 1460 and was fought in the water meadows south of the river Nene close by Delapre. King Henry arrayed his army on the pastures with backs to the river. The earls came over the high ground from Hardingstone and, with the advantage of position, slaughtered the royal force. The river was said to have run red with blood, ten thousand men being either hacked down or drowned. Henry was brought prisoner to Northampton and later deposed.

Queen Elizabeth I made at least three state visits to Northampton. For her first, in the summer of 1564, the whole town was repainted and profusely decorated, the roadways strewn with flower petals. The citizens presented her with a gift of a fine embroidered purse that alone cost six guineas and which contained £20 in coin. A similar sum was allotted for the mayor to arrange a programme of public entertainment that included bull and bear baiting. In 1575 she again passed through the town, on her way to stay at the palace of Holdenby, a few miles to the north.

When Charles I came to the throne Northampton was at first supportive. When he set out to quell the Irish rebellion the town supplied his army with 4,600 pairs of boots. However, when civil war broke out Northampton, with its Protestant background, supported the Parliamentarians. Throughout the conflict Northampton, being on the crossroads of England, was constantly playing host to regiments of Cromwell's army, a continuing drain on the town's resources. After the final and decisive battle of the Civil War, at Naseby in 1645, Charles was incarcerated at nearby Holdenby, frequently being allowed to visit Northampton to play bowls in the meantime. On 2 June 1647 he was taken from there, through the town to the ringing of bells, to his execution in London.

In 1649 a band of mutineers from the New Army, calling themselves Levellers, led by a man named Thomson, seized control of Northampton, terrorised the mayor and authorities, and plundered the exchequer, before being pursued and killed by troops.

It was during Cromwell's Protectorate that Northampton's dissenting tendencies were firmly established and the foundations of nonconformity laid. Upon the restoration of the monarchy Charles II saw the town as a threat, with its strong fortifications and its freethinking citizens, and ordered the demolition of the castle in 1662.

Fire was always a great danger in cramped towns and Northampton suffered several serious outbreaks. That of Monday, 20 September 1675 was the worst. It broke out in St Mary's Street at noon and rapidly spread in a semicircle around the town, thanks to a veering wind. In the space of six hours it had devoured over 600 houses, made 700 families homeless, and claimed the lives of 11 townsmen. The town was left a smoking ruin, damage being assessed at £250,000 including £50,000 for All Saints' Church which was totally destroyed. Only one building that predates the Great Fire still exists in Northampton—Hazelrigg House, in Marefair.

Northampton's reputation as a stronghold of dissension was reinforced in the 18th century when the Rev. Dr. Philip Doddridge set up his academy, reckoned to be among the leading educational establishments of its time. In 1729 he became minister of Castle Hill Chapel, giving a considerable boost to a community which had been established there since 1662. It has been said that Northampton's independence of political and religious principles stems from the fact that shoemaking was the craft of outworkers. Each craftsman had his own workshop or room at home and made his own special contribution to the construction of a shoe. Components and part-finished footwear were transported about the streets from workshop to workshop in baskets until completed. The craftsmen were, in effect, self employed, independent and obliged to no single employer.

This independence was never demonstrated more forcefully than in the matter of Charles Bradlaugh, the radical M.P. Several times he was ejected from the House of Commons for refusing to take the oath upon the Bible. Further elections were held and again Bradlaugh won the day and, then as now, M.P.s were allowed to aver, rather than swear, if they so wished. A fine 7ft. 6in. Doulton statue of the politician now graces Abington Square.

Queen Victoria paid only one brief visit to Northampton during her 64-year reign. In 1844, having disembarked from the train at Weedon, the nearest railway station at that time, and on her way to Burghley House, home of the Marquess of Exeter, she paused outside the *George Inn* to hear a loyal address by the mayor. In her honour a medical practice was set up for the poorer townsfolk and named the Royal Victoria Dispensary.

The year before this royal visit the first recorded photographic studio was set up in Northampton's Mercers' Row, offering Beards Patent Daguerreotype Portraits at one guinea each, colouring 2s. 6d. extra. The process was of little use for recording the town's appearance or the royal visit, however, for it was so slow that movement made images of people and animals simply disappear.

At this time the population of the town was approaching 22,000 and Northampton was firmly established as the leading centre of the footwear industry. It was also a thriving market town serving a wealthy agricultural community. The London, North Western Railway opened its Peterborough line at Cotton End to serve it.

Education took a leap forward in 1845 when the British School built new three-roomed premises next door to the gaol on the Mounts.

The borough gaol was also opened in 1845 with accommodation for 94 male and 16 female prisoners. Taking a cue from this, a new county gaol was also constructed in St Giles's Square to replace a grim former prison on the site, and opened in 1846.

In 1863 one of Northampton's most famous landmarks was erected on the Market Square. Samuel Isaacs, a local shoe manufacturer, presented the town with a fine fountain. Cast at a local foundry, the iron column, with granite base, four fountains playing into bowls, drinking fountains, cattle troughs and ornate gas lanterns, was designed to mark the marriage of Prince Albert Edward, the Prince of Wales, to Princess Alexandra of Denmark. For almost a full century it was the pride of Northamptonians until the corporation declared it unfit and had it demolished in 1962. The matter still rankles among older natives.

Cattle, sheep and farm produce were sold on the Square until July 1873 when the weekly disruption finally forced the move to a new purpose-built five-acre cattle market by the river.

The town was expanding fast and changing rapidly. The population in 1851 stood at 26,658, by 1861 it was 32,813 and, by 1871, 41,168. Although not on the main line, a loop from Roade to Rugby brought the railway to the Castle station in 1859. The Midland station at St John's Street was built in 1872, making a stylish terminus for the Bedford line which had been opened in 1866.

The blossoming town demanded a larger and more suitable town hall. The old building which had stood at the corner of Abington Street and Wood Hill since the 13th century was inconvenient and, by now, ramshackle. An imposing new edifice was designed by E.W. Godwin and the foundation stone laid in 1861. It was opened in May of 1864 by the mayor, Councillor Mark Dorman. The first extension, designed in a superbly sensitive style by Matthew Holding, was opened in 1892. For anyone interested in the history of Northampton this building is a storybook in stone. Highly ornate, it is decorated with hundreds of carved scenes depicting incidents in the town's history, figures from local legends, crafts, sports and so on. Some even depict nursery rhymes and fables familiar to local children. A further extension, suitably sympathetic in design, has been completed in recent years and houses modern sculpture.

In recent years Northampton's staple industry of boot and shoe making, and its associated leather crafts, have dwindled and all but died. Traditionally footwear had been handmade for centuries, but the Industrial Revolution introduced machines that were capable of taking over some of the tasks involved. By 1820 there were at least 18 wholesale shoe manufacturers in the town, despite much of the work still being done by outworkers—men, women and very young children—in their own homes. As the century wore on mechanisation increased until most of a shoe's construction could be done by machine. The town was home to many huge factories, its air was permeated with the smell of well-tanned leather and punctuated by the rat-a-tat-tat of stitching machines or the scream of edge-trimmers. Right up until the Second World War Northampton retained its reputation for quality footwear; indeed, the local saying was 'It's as right as leather!'. Sadly, shoemaking has declined since the war, caused by the import of cheap footwear from the Far East and eastern bloc countries. Odd pockets of handsewn craftsmanship still survive, though, its products commanding high prices and being sought by discerning customers throughout the world.

In its heyday Northampton was a wealthy town, a town of full employment, liberal facilities and fine buildings. In the aftermath of the Second World War, and in the scramble of municipal authorities to cash in on the redevelopment boom, major destruction of old buildings took place. The New Theatre, the Emporium Arcade, St John's Street station and the Notre Dame Convent, School and Chapel, as well as innumerable less important, but nonetheless attractive, properties were wiped out to make way for shopping complexes and offices, many of which remain empty.

Now, it would appear, the town is coming back to life. Its position at the cross-roads of the country makes it an ideal distribution site, and many and varied are the firms which maintain warehouses here. For the same reason light industry finds Northampton a convenient place to establish operations.

OUT AND ABOUT

1 The Drapery in the 1890s looking northwards from George Row. The name The Drapery, which today is used for this entire thoroughfare, properly applies to only the west side. The east side is The Glovery. On the right can be seen the railings around All Saints' Church.

2 An amazing construction of timber and ropes forms the scaffolding for the buildings of the Westminster Bank premises on the corner of The Drapery and Mercers' Row in 1925. Stonework was by local masons White and Joyce whose model T Ford truck can be seen on the left. The 45-ft. circumference copper dome which surmounted the new building was considered a handsome addition to the town centre.

3 Electric trams were introduced into the town in 1904 and here, about 1908, we see an open-topped tram picking up passengers at the bottom of The Drapery. Advertised on the front of the tram, Higgins was a firm of haberdashers and drapers which occupied premises on The Parade until after the Second World War. The awning to the left of the tram, bearing the inscription 'Nothing over 6½d' was outside Cooley's Bazaar.

4 Looking southwards down The Drapery, the *George Hotel* can be seen in the far distance. Adnitt Bros., on the right, traded as high quality drapers and lady's outfitters until being taken over by Debenhams in recent years.

5 The *George Hotel*, on the corner of George Row and Bridge Street, was demolished in 1921 and Lloyd's Bank was erected on the site. An inn had occupied this site for many centuries, the earliest record dating from 1555. Viewed from Bridge Street, in the foreground is the small door that led to a men-only tap-room known as the *Hole in the Wall*.

6 On the south side of George Row is the County Hall which includes the courts and sessions house. Designed by amateur architect Sir Roger Norwich and finished in 1682, it is an outstanding example of Corinthian style. Some of the masonry exhibits a curious pink tinge. Stacks of dressed stone, awaiting construction, were affected by the heat of the Great Fire in 1675, and the exposed blocks changed colour.

7 Derngate, once known as Swyneswell and then Waterloo, was an important artery for the town in medieval times. By Victorian times it had become lined with stylish town houses. On the left, in the middle distance, is the arched entrance to Albion Place, a private enclave of fine residences.

8 Abington Street, seen from the Market Square corner in the 1890s, was a narrow, winding thoroughfare. The site occupied by grocer C. Holyoak was known by later generations as either Doffman's Corner, the 'fifty bob tailor's', or John Collier's, after the various businesses that used it. The *Three Tuns Inn*, part of which can be seen on the left, was only one of ten public houses that surrounded the Market Square at this time.

9 Abington Street widened as one travelled eastward. Where Wellington Street joined it, on the right, stood the grand, domed offices of the Northampton Gas Light Company. Approaching the photographer is a fine little De Dion Bouton motorcar, the most reliable vehicle of its type at that time.

10 The view eastwards along Abington Street, *c*.1910. In the distance is the convent of Notre Dame and, nearer, the small opening of Albert Place. On the right can be seen the cobbled entrance that once led, in the days of horse-drawn trams, to the stables in Grooms Yard.

11 Abington Square, where Abington Street divides to become the Kettering and Wellingborough Roads. The statue of Charles Bradlaugh, the radical Northampton M.P., which was erected in 1894, stands before the building which housed the People's Restaurant and Billiard Hall, a refreshment house run by the Blue Ribbon temperance organisation for the benefit of working men. The building was demolished to make way for the Garden of Rest.

12 Heavy snowfall in the winter of 1946 leaves the road in front of All Saints' Church treacherous for traffic. Corporation workmen clear the snow and remove it with one of the Allchin steam lorries made locally at the South Bridge factory.

13 Looking along Wood Hill from an upper window of the Judge's Lodgings on a busy market day in the 1890s. The public house *The Old Duke of Clarence* was a direct descendant of an inn called the *Queen's Dragoon* in existence there in 1676. It later became the *Leg of Mutton* before acquiring its new name in 1814. It closed in 1911 when the structure became unsafe. Parade House, in the distance, was demolished to make way for the Emporium Arcade, erected in 1908 and demolished in 1972.

14 The Emporium Arcade can be seen just left of the pillar in this view from the tower of All Saints' Church in the 1930s. Next door was Abel's, established as a bookshop in 1794 but better known later as a music shop, gaining the royal warrant to Queen Victoria in 1846 and to the Prince of Wales in 1863. The business closed in 1970. To the left is J. & G. Higgins, haberdasher.

15 Welsh House at the bottom of Newland, once known as Dr. Danver's House, survived the Great Fire of Northampton in 1675 and was the escape route for local folk surrounded by flame in the Market Square. Now known as Welsh House from the motto that adorns the front 'Heb Dyw Heb Dwya Digon' (Without God, without everything; with God, enough) and the arms of the Williams of Penrhyn.

16 The northern end of Newland looking back across the Lady's Lane opening. Despite its name, Newland is one of the oldest thoroughfares in the town. During medieval times it contained many dormitories housing the students of the friars, several orders of which had establishments in the area.

17 Running westward from the town centre is Gold Street. When this photograph was taken *c*.1908 several deliveries were being made by drays from the London & North Western and the London, Midland & Scottish railways. The police constable standing dreamily in the middle of the road is about to get a rude awakening from one of the new-fangled motorcars approaching from Marefair.

18 In the 1890s the north side of Marefair was occupied by Parkinson the photographer, who had recently expanded from a studio in Gold Street, and a tumbledown old inn called the *Rose and Punchbowl*.

19 The old *Rose and Punchbowl* pub had been demolished and rebuilt as an hotel by the time of this photograph in about 1902. The entire north side of Marefair had also been developed. Soon after the *Rose and Punchbowl Hotel* was bought by the railway company and renamed the *North Western Hotel*.

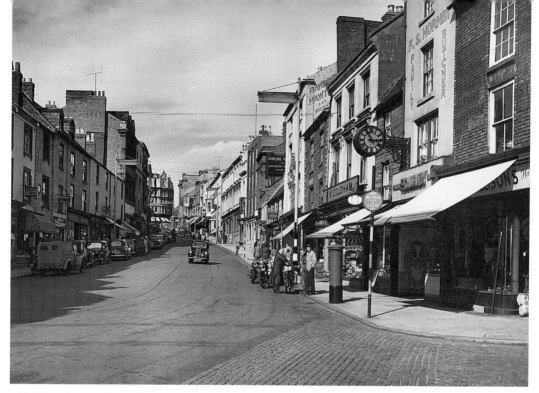

20 Running southwards from All Saints', Bridge Street has always been the main route into and out of Northampton leading, as it still does, to the London road. The entire right-hand side of this picture, taken in the 1960s, has now been redeveloped. Coldham's bicycle and motorcycle shop collapsed to rubble and never re-opened. The premises of Dennis Willison, a saddler, on the right was demolished to widen the roadway for a one-way traffic scheme.

21 Between the Cotton End level crossing and Ransome Road (a site now occupied by a Co-op supermarket) was a jumble of workshops partly hidden by hoardings. A curious local landmark here was a building owned by a slaughterer and knacker. On the side of the wall were exhibited two giant elephant skulls, acquired during his work for the local Fosset's Circus.

22 The road through Far Cotton that led to Towcester was called St Leonard's Road after a hospital and leper house that once stood nearby. Here we see the horse bus turning in the road. Although the terminus was actually at St Mary's Church, we can assume that Mr. Christy, who owned the grocery shop on the left, had bribed the bus driver to turn his vehicle so that the photographer caught the advertisement for Christy's Tea!

23 Primrose Hill, the continuation of Barrack Road towards Kingsthorpe Hollow, as an electric tram sails gracefully by the junction with Freehold Street.

24 The view from gardens at the end of Freehold Street looking towards the distant trees of Thornton's Park. In the nearby hollow, Balfour Road has not yet been driven through the smallholdings, although Stanhope Road and Cranbrook Road can be seen, with the *Halfway House* public house beyond.

25 Kingsthorpe Hollow. The terrace on the left is punctuated by Alpha Street, on the corner of which is the *Spotted Dog* pub, and beyond it the *Victoria Tavern*, while opposite are other pubs, the *White Lion* and the *Freehold Arms*.

LOST LANDMARKS

26 The largest and probably the most important structure to have been lost to the town is Northampton Castle. It was sold to the London, North Western Railway Company by Samuel Walker for £15,000 in the 1870s. Built by Simon de Senlis, a Norman knight in the 11th century, it became an important administrative centre. Four parliaments were held here, poll tax was first introduced from here, and an Act for Scottish Independence was announced here. The trial of Thomas à Becket and his subsequent escape is probably the highlight of the castle's history. The postern gate, seen here, is the only fragment that has survived, albeit as an almost unrecognisable Victorian rebuild.

27 The fountain on the Market Square was a foca
point for gatherings of all kinds. Its steps saw speaker:
of all kinds, protests, proclamations and preachers
Erected in 1863 to mark the marriage of Princ
Albert Edward, Prince of Wales, to Princes:
Alexandra of Denmark, it was the private gift of Mr
Samuel Isaacs, a local shoe factory owner. Here a
political speaker of the National Party prepares to
address his supporters from a loudspeaker van in the
run-up to the 1935 General Election.

28 In the 1960s great changes were taking place ii
the town and the corporation was planning to
reorganise the market. Claiming that the structur
was dangerous, they ordered the fountain to b
demolished. Work commenced on 15 April 1962
Despite its alleged weakness, the fountain require(
cranes, cutting torches, a team of hefty workme:
and two days' hard work to remove it.

29 A well-known landmark in Wood Hill was Eckford's kiosk. The little newspaper stand had started off immediately after the First World War in front of All Saints' Church. Mr. Eckford had returned from the war minus one leg and wanted to set up this kiosk. Opposition from established newsagents was resisted by vigorous popular support and a public petition, and the objectors were overruled. It remained there until alterations to the pavement area forced its move.

30 The *Northampton Mercury* is the oldest continuously published newspaper in the country, never having missed an edition since its establishment in 1720. At the time of this picture of its Market Square premises, it had not yet merged with its rival paper the *Herald*, which had been started in 1831. The *Echo* also subsequently merged with the *Chronicle*, a paper that dated from 1880. Among the films being advertised by the many cinemas was 'For Valour' and 'Buck Privates', supported by Rin-Tin-Tin, at the Temperance Hall, Norma Talmage in 'The Dove' and Charles Warren in 'Lost at the Front' at the Majestic, and 'The King's Flame' at the Vaudeville, Grove Road.

31 In Abington Street was the New Theatre, known to generations of Northamptonians as 'The Hipp' or Hippodrome. It opened in 1912 and survived until the curtain fell on the last show in 1958. The theatre was demolished two years later.

32 The painting over the proscenium arch, seen here exposed during the demolition of the New Theatre, was saved by local historian Dr. Reynolds, but was stolen along with other memorabilia during a burglary upon his death.

33 The old Borough Gaol on the Mounts was a grim landmark that dated from 1845. Originally it housed 100 inmates but over the years it was gradually extended and modernised until, in 1929, it was purchased by the council and demolished soon after to make way for a new police headquarters and fire station. Seven murderers had been executed and buried at the prison, the last in 1914. Their bodies were removed at dead of night and reinterred at Towcester Road cemetery.

34 The *Peacock Hotel* on the Market Square was an inn with a fine coachyard and a history traceable to 1456. The entire building was demolished in 1960 to make way for a modern office block that was so hideous that it, too, was demolished to allow the construction of the present Peacock Arcade shopping mall.

35 In Sheep Street was the raised pavement known as Locock's Hill. The Locock family, whose residence this was
were all medical men, one of whom was *accoucheur* to Queen Victoria and present at the birth of all of her children
The room over the porch, known as The Observatory, and the 'hill', which allowed Dr. Locock to step straight intc
his carriage, were demolished in 1927. In later years the building became a Bedding Centre, but has recently beer
restored as a prestige office block.

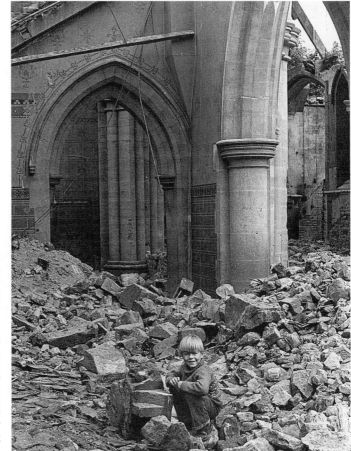

36 St Edmund's Church, on the Wellingborough road, was erected in 1850 and demolished in 1980. The original and ancient St Edmund's Church once stood just outside the town's east gate, where Abington Square now is, and dated back to Norman times.

37 The British School, with teaching along the lines of the Lancastrian schools, was started in Derngate in 1812, but moved here to Campbell Square in 1846. In 1870 it was enlarged to become an important school in 1880 when school attendance was made compulsory. In later years it became the highly regarded Campbell Square Intermediate School. Upon closure it served for a while as local government offices before being demolished to create a car park.

Industry and Commerce

38 *(Below)* Northampton has for centuries been famous for leather, particularly its boots and shoes. In the closing room, as here at Barratt's in 1931, the various parts that form the uppers are stitched together and the shoe begins to take familiar shape.

39 *(Above right)* The final stage of shoemaking is in the finishing room where the completed footwear is trimmed, buffed and polished. This is Manfield's model factory some time before the First World War.

40 *(Below right)* Another aspect of leathercraft is bookbinding. Birdsall's, in Wood Street, was a large firm that had a new factory constructed in 1888. As can be seen in this photograph, much of the work was done by hand.

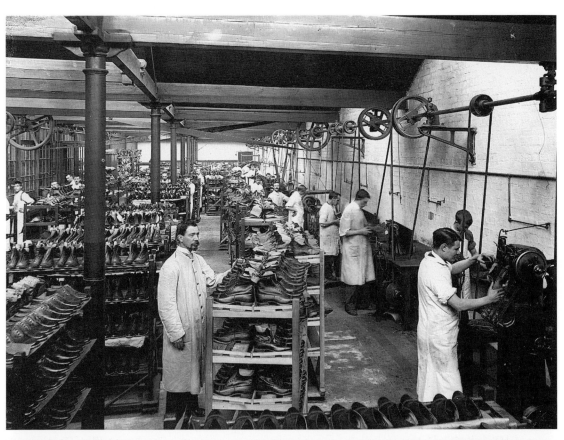

41 Trimming the bound leaves was done by guillotine, the machines operated by girls and boys as young as twelve.

42 The final binding and the hand-tooling with gold leaf were done by highly-skilled craftsmen.

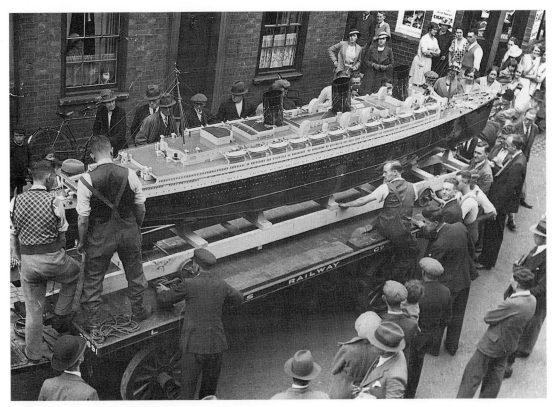

43 Northampton is also well known throughout the world as the home of Bassett-Lowke Ltd. the model-makers. A fine model of the liner *Queen Mary* is loaded on a railway dray to begin its journey to the U.S.A. in 1936.

44 Another product of the Bassett-Lowke factory, an impressive waterline model of the *Empress of Britain*. Made for the Canadian Pacific Railway Company in 1930, it was 21 feet long. A last minute decision to mount the model on a float for display as part of the Lord Mayor's Show in London left craftsmen only eight days to construct the model. Working day and night they completed it in time. The real ship had been launched by the Prince of Wales in June 1930. One of its unusual features was the cocktail bar which was designed by Heath Robinson!

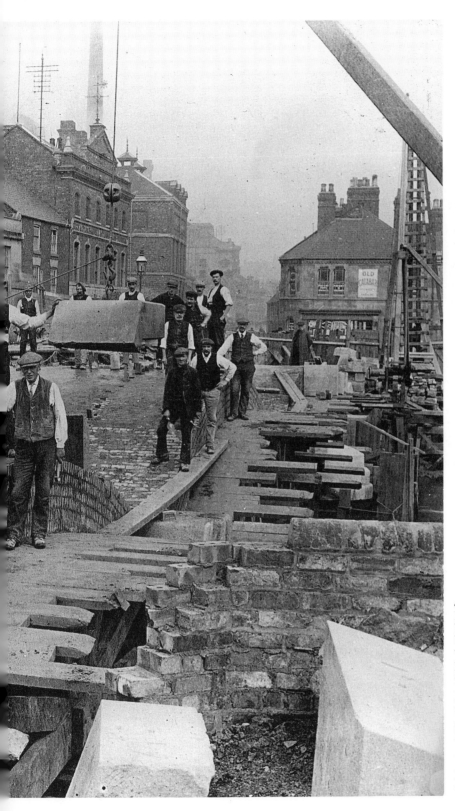

45 In 1912 the South Bridge, which for years had been something of a bottleneck on the road south, was widened by 20 feet preparatory to commencing an electric tram service to Far Cotton. The warehouse on the extreme left was burned down in recent years soon after being declared a listed building. Beyond the *Crown and Anchor* pub can be seen Rice's foundry, later to move to South Bridge Road.

46 William Osborn, who had commenced business in Adelaide Street, moved to open these premises on the Earl Street/Upper Mounts corner where the *Chronicle & Echo* building now stands. Advertised on the left is Colman's Sinapisms, a type of mustard plaster. On the right is the *Black Boy* pub, one of two with that name in the town.

47 *(Top right)* Another member of the Osborn family joined forces with William Pitts, a fellow grocer from St Giles' Street, and took this house at 21 Sheep Street for conversion to a shop. On the left is the *Ram Hotel*.

48 *(Bottom right)* Pitts & Osborn's after the alterations, displaying a stylish shopfront with one window stacked with marmalades and chutneys, the other with soaps such as Hydroleine, Hudson's Dry Soap, Sunlight and Venus.

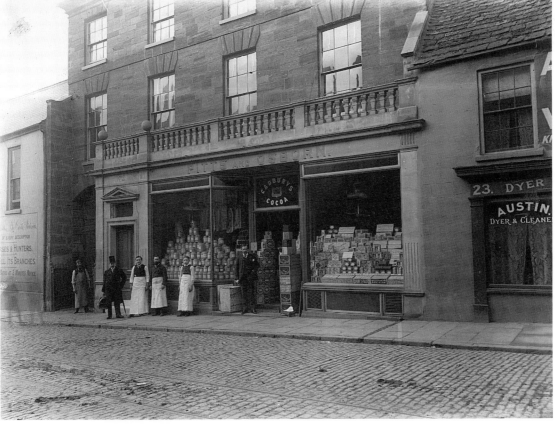

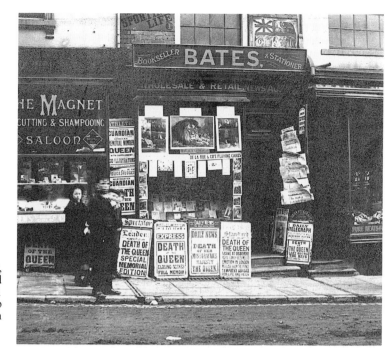

49 James Bates, at 3 Bridge Street, was a newsagent who also sold books, prints and postcards. In 1901 the placards outside his shop announced the death of Queen Victoria.

50 Where have all the errand-boys gone? Youths like this butcher's boy with his delivery basket, posing outside Cotton's shop in Bearward Street, were a common sight, whistling as they went on their rounds.

51 *(Far right)* Frederick R. Robbins was a fishmonger, poulterer and game dealer with a shop on the Wellingborough road. However, at Christmas time the shop was decked out completely with plucked birds. Few homes boasted ice-boxes and refrigerators were almost unheard of, so most birds were collected on Christmas Eve. To save you counting, there are 259 carcases hanging here!

THE SUBURBS

52 St James's End was not originally part of Northampton but was a hamlet divided between the parishes of Dallington and Duston. Much of the land had belonged to the black friars of St James's Abbey which had stood here since the 11th century. Café Square, so-called after the Althorp Café seen here, forms the junction of the Harlestone and Weedon roads. In this picture, taken *c.*1910, the church can be seen without its tower. This was added after the First World War as a memorial to the fallen.

53 The view from outside St James's Church looking towards the Weedon road, *c*.1911. Just beyond the post office can be seen the *Tramcar Tavern*. Just round the corner, out of sight, was another pub, the *Florence Nightingale*.

54 Dallington village was absorbed into the town in 1932 and was, like the hall seen here which was the residence of Viscount Althorp, all once owned by the Spencers. The hall later became the Margaret Spencer Convalescent Home, served as a hospital during the last war, and is now split into flats. The land shown here was an idyllic area of lakes, waterfalls and arbours, later to become the Dallington Lawn Tennis Club.

55 Duston, too, has now been absorbed into Northampton borough, although it successfully resisted until 1965. In this view, dated *c*.1895, we see cattle being driven past the *Squirrel Inn*.

56 Kingsthorpe village, once a royal estate attached to the palace at Moulton Park, in the 1890s. The lane is The Leys, looking northwards towards what is now Vicarage Lane. The village was absorbed by Northampton borough in 1900.

57 Kingsthorpe Mill was the middle one of three watermills on this stretch of the river. Long after the mill was demolished the road, known as Mill Lane, twisted to cross the infant river Nene. The old mill race was later concreted to form a bathing place. Now, though, the whole site has been obliterated by the construction of a busy ring road.

58 Even the far-flung village of Moulton is now swallowed up by Northampton's hungry maw. The *Shoulder of Mutton* was only one of at least seven pubs and inns in the village.

59 High Street, Weston Favell, now within the borough boundary. The quaint, thatched *Horse Shoe Inn* was later knocked down and rebuilt as a brick, mock-Tudor pub, but has recently been swept away for housing development.

GETTING ABOUT

60 Mr. Robert Frisby, who kept the *Peacock Hotel* and who came from a family of horsemasters, kept up the tradition of coaching. A member of the Four in Hand Club, etc., he ran the 'Old Times' coach and many horse-drawn carriages right into the 1930s. Upon his death in 1937 the 'Old Times' was sold to Bertram Mills, the circus owner.

61 Dressed for the part, Mr. Frisby and friends with the 'Old Times' at Epsom for the Derby.

62 The first proper ambulance in the town was manned by members of the Northampton Ambulance Corps and is seen outside the Northampton General Hospital. It replaced a hand-pushed two-wheeled litter. Earlier still, patients had to make their way to hospital as best they could. One man, for instance, badly mauled in the bearpit at Franklin's Gardens, is recorded as having been pushed on a handcart by a policeman the three miles through the streets.

63 The Northampton Street Tramway Company commenced operation in 1881 with horse-drawn trams. Car number 15 is seen at the Café Square terminus at St James's End. This car was involved in a serious accident on Saturday, 20 April 1901, when it ran away down Abington Street and overturned at Wood Hill, injuring 20 passengers, one fatally.

64 In 1904 the Corporation, having bought the old Street Tramway Co. for £37,000, decided to electrify the system. The town, as here in Marefair, was torn apart for the laying of the new tracks. A knot of interested spectators stands left outside the *North Western Hotel*. The Palace of Varieties occupies the corner of Gold Street and Horseshoe Street while the *Shakespeare Inn* is on the right.

65 Further afield the tracks headed for one terminus at the *Kingsley Park Hotel*. In the Kettering road, near the top of Portland Street, workmen lay a double track at a passing place.

66 On the day of the inauguration of the electric tram service on 21 July 1904 a decorated car passes through St James's End. The photographer, in fact, has his back to the undertaking's purpose-built depot, known generally as the 'tram sheds'. On the first Saturday, 27,000 used the new trams and on the Sunday another 15,000.

67 Even though the rest of the town was served by electric trams from 1904, Far Cotton had to make do with a horse bus service until 1914. This, the very last horse bus to run before giving way to electric, waits for passengers outside the *Clinton Arms*, on the Towcester road.

68 In 1914, the problems of traversing the railway level crossing at Cotton End being solved, tracks were laid to Far Cotton. Here at Cotton End, where the old Towcester road joins London Road just south of South Bridge, the new tracks prepare to converge before crossing the bridge.

69 The first aeroplane to be seen by most Northamptonians was the Bleriot craft flown by pioneer aviator Will Moorhouse, who lived at Spratton Grange, just north of the town. In October 1911, having only been flying for three weeks and having acquired his pilot's licence only the day before, he landed his plane on the Racecourse on his way home, bringing the town to a virtual standstill as people rushed to see this new means of travel.

70 The next day he landed again to collect three pairs of Barratt's shoes for transport to Hendon—the first ever aerial delivery service. Taking off with difficulty behind his 50-horsepower Gnome engine, he flew southwards at 75 mph. Finding thick fog at Fenny Stratford, he was forced to land, to continue his journey the next day. It thus took two days to deliver the shoes! During the First World War Moorhouse served with the Royal Flying Corps, was fatally injured in a bombing raid on Courtrai on 26 April 1915 and became the first ever pilot to be awarded the Victoria Cross.

71 In 1912 another pioneer aviator, Henri Salmet, who was touring the country giving flying displays with the backing of the *Daily Mail*, landed on the Racecourse. During the day he gave demonstrations with his Bleriot monoplane.

72 *(Top left)* A famous figure among pioneer motorcyclists was the vicar of the Holy Sepulchre Church, Rev. Basil H. Davies, who wrote books and regular magazine columns under the nom-de-plume of 'Ixion'. He is seen with his curate, another motorcycle enthusiast Rev. Percy W. Bischoff. The pair are preparing their machines for the 1911 Scottish Six Days Trial. Davies' machine is a Rudge fitted with NSU gears, while Bischoff's is a 499cc Triumph. Bischoff left the church in 1919 to take up employment with the Clyno motorcycle factory.

73 *(Bottom left)* A friend and colleague of Ixion was local leather manufacturer and inventor of slot machines, Albert E. Catt. After creating a long distance record in 1910, he set out the following year to beat it and to set the record beyond reach of challengers. He rode his Triumph, belt-driven motorcycle for six days, covering an amazing 2,557 miles. At the finish at Becket's Well he was welcomed by the mayor, etc. and a great crowd of enthusiasts. He was so exhausted physically, his legs and arms swollen with the battering, that he had to be lifted from his machine.

74 *(Above)* Albert Catt junior, son of the long distance record breaker, was also a motorcycling celebrity in his own right. Here he prepares his Scott twin two-stroke racing machine for the 1923 Amateur T.T. race in the Isle of Man. His mechanic is Arthur Kinch, a local tuning wizard. Note the strap-on knee grips on the tank, necessary for the bumpy T.T. circuit, and the spare inner tube, already partly inflated to save valuable time, wrapped round the rider's waist.

75 During the First World War many local lads enlisted as despatch riders using their own machines. Three of this group are riding Triumphs, found to be so reliable in service that they came to be known as 'Trustys'. One, NH1424, is a Rudge Multi, a bike with the luxury of infinitely variable gearing, much on the lines of a modern Daf car.

76 Family travel, if you could afford it, was often by means of an old sidecar outfit. Mr. and Mrs. Richards of Kingsthorpe load their six children into the side-car of the single-cylinder B.S.A. for an outing in the mid-1930s. The bike was already at least ten years old at this time.

77 The first ever petrol filling station was introduced at Aldermaston, near Newbury, in the winter of 1919/20 by the Automobile Association and before long they had mushroomed all over the country. At Far Cotton F. & E. Beedens had soon set up a filling station alongside their garage. Pratt's, B.P., Shellmex, and Power were among the brands sold at 1s. 4d. and 1s. 7d. a gallon.

78 A few hundred yards south, on the London road, was another filling station. The Dennis lorry, operated by Dixon's and loaded with locally made joinery, used to make a twice weekly journey to Cornwall and back, an arduous trip on the cast-iron wheels and solid rubber tyres fitted.

79 Joseph Grose was the first person to own a motor car in Northampton, running a Coventry Motette in 1896. He is seen here astride an ABC Skootamota, one of a number of scooter-style vehicles introduced just after the First World War. The Skootamota was made by the Sopwith aeroplane company.

80 During the First World War soldiers home on leave often arrived at Castle station after the trams had ceased to run. To assist them, a group of local people subscribed £100 to buy a secondhand model T Ford for the Special Constabulary, so that they could operate a 'get-you-home' service.

81 Shortage of petrol during the First World War forced operators of commercial vehicles to look for other solutions. Beeden's charabanc, picking up passengers from the *Princess Alexandra* pub in Alexandra Road, carries a gas bag on its roof. Coal-gas was an unsatisfactory alternative being inefficient and bulky, but was unrationed. Quoted running costs equated to 6d. a gallon.

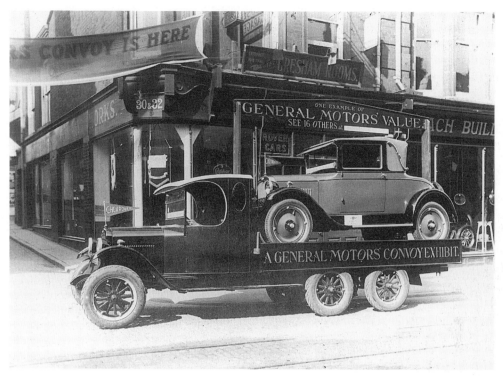

82 Grose's garage grew into a large business that spread into Marefair along Pike Lane and through to Horsemarket. By 1928 it had become agent for the giant General Motors, as well as for many other makers. As part of an advertising campaign a Chevrolet two-seater with dickey is displayed on a Chevrolet flat-bed truck.

83 A miniature Vauxhall car attracts a small crowd on the Market Square in November 1934.   The little one-horse-power vehicle, capable of 12 miles an hour, was based on a Rytecraft machine and travelled the country as an advertising gimmick.

84 Traffic accidents were not uncommon. A well-known blackspot was (and still is) the junction of Birchfield Road and Park Avenue North where we see two cars, a Model T Ford and a Morris Minor, overturned in a collision. The incident occurred on Good Friday 1931 and the Ford was loaded with hot cross buns. The Morris Saloon was owned by a house decorator and he and three youths in his employ were drenched in whitewash being carried in buckets.

85   Mr. J. Hollingsworth had started as a carriage and coachbuilder in Northampton in 1876 and succeeded in business incorporating his own inventions, special pole and bar attachments, new forms of cee-springs and patent wheels. By the time we see the firm here at the 1926 Northampton County Show it was at the peak of its success, supplying 'everything for the motorist'. The vehicle on the left is a Morris 14-cwt travellers coupe; that on the right is a 15-cwt Ford model T van. In later years Hollingsworth's specialised in automobile electrics.

86 In 1910 the town bought its first motor fire engine, replacing the old horse-drawn steamer. To placate those who reckoned this an unwarranted expense, a display was mounted on the market square. The vehicle, a Merryweather costing £1,272, was named the 'T.L. Wright' and was capable of putting up two 200-ft. jets.

87 The demonstration was watched closely by the Mayor, Ald. H. Butterfield, seen on the left.

88 1936 and the fire brigade was still under the command of the chief constable, John Williamson (centre). The old motor engine had been replaced by a new pump escape.

89 The brigade, though, was still using the old fire station in Dychurch Lane, a relic of the old horse-drawn volunteer fire brigade days. A 'shout', a term still used for a turn-out by firemen that dates back to horse-drawn days when drivers needed to use both hands so had a distinctive shout to warn of their approach, was still an exciting sight and was enough to attract a small group of spectators to witness the scene. The site of the station is now occupied by the new Town Hall extension.

90 At the end of the Second World War, the fire brigade, still under the regulation of the National Fire Service, helps to set Cleaver's clock in Abington Street going once more. Note the street lamp that still carries its blackout mask, as does the fire engine.

91 Just about the last horses routinely to work Northampton's streets were those of the L.M.S. railway company. The horse Joe, seen here, was due to be sent to the knacker's yard, but a public outcry and a subscription list sent him instead to a farm at King's Sutton to live out his remaining days.

ABINGTON PARK

92 Abington Manor was once home to Shakespeare's favourite granddaughter Elizabeth Hall. Then, after serving as home to the Thursby family for almost two hundred years, it became a private mental asylum for a while before being given to the town by Lord and Lady Wantage in 1892. The estate was opened as a public park in 1897, marking the diamond jubilee of Queen Victoria.

93 In the days of private occupancy Abington Manor employed a large outdoor staff of gardeners, nurserymen and estate workers.

94 The main body of the church of SS Peter and Paul at Abington was rebuilt in 1821. The gated lane in this picture, which dates from the 1890s, is now Park Avenue South. The sunken wall, or ha-ha, was designed to keep grazing cattle out of the ornamental garden.

95 The main portion of the 116-acre estate was put to grazing, let out to a tenant. The farm buildings, nowadays used as park offices and stores, are often referred to as Cockerill's Farm after a former occupant.

96 When it was decided to open the park to the public much of the ancient walling was removed and replaced with iron railings. Workmen pause for the photographer, while the foreman and the park keeper take pride of place on the left.

97 The cottages and stables on the main Wellingborough road, commonly called Archway Cottages, were part of the manor's estate. During the 1930s the corporation proposed to pull them down in a road straightening scheme, but a vigorous preservation campaign led by Tom Osborne Robinson, the scenic designer at the Royal Theatre, successfully saved them. Suggestions were then made to turn the buildings into a rural museum, but this idea came to nothing. The buildings still survive and, after recent restoration, are still lived in.

CALLED TO THE BAR

98 Northampton has always been well endowed with inns, public houses and taverns. It seemed that almost every corner had its beerhouse or pub. One of the grander establishments was the *Kingsley Park Hotel*. Built in 1883 to serve the racing fraternity visiting the nearby Racecourse, it was left out on a limb when racing ceased in 1904 and it became known locally as the 'white elephant'. After over half a century it acquired the name 'White Elephant' officially. Following a brief spell as the *Kingsley Park Tavern* it has again reverted to the *White Elephant*.

99 *(Top right)* The *Cock Inn* at Kingsthorpe stood near a section of road known as the Tollbar. As both the Welford and the Harborough roads were turnpikes, a tollhouse and bar controlled the road at this point. In more recent years the old inn was rebuilt as a grander sandstone building and became the *Cock Hotel*.

100 *(Bottom right)* Just across the road from the *Cock Inn* was *The White Horse*, premises that served jointly as a pub run by Fanny Dix and a workshop for her husband John. Although he advertised himself as an ornamental plasterer, he probably also brewed beer for the pub, for he had earlier practised the art in premises in Broad Street.

101 The *Angel Hotel* in Bridge Street was a long-established coaching inn.

102 Almost opposite the *Angel* was *The Saddlers' Arms*, better known among locals as Old Dan Muscutt's. Sausage and mash with bread was available for 3½d., while good English roast beef mutton, or pork, freshly cut from hot joints, was served with two vegetables and Yorkshire pudding for 6d., 9d. or 1s.

103 Also in Bridge Street but further south, close by the railway level crossing, was the *Old White Hart Inn*. After a rebuild it continued as a pub until utilised by the Watney Mann brewery firm as a social club for its workers.

104 *(Top left) The Lord Palmerston*, on the Market Square, changed its name from the *Flying Horse* in honour of the great statesman when his wife came to the area to open Towcester railway station in 1864. In 1973 it changed its name to the *Lamplighter* but closed in 1980. Today it is a fast-food bar. H. Goulston, the licensee at the time this photograph was taken, was a tramway expert who originally was brought to Northampton to oversee the establishment of the old Street Tramway Company. The pub next door, the *Post Horn*, was reputed to be the hangout of local villains.

105 *(Bottom left)* It was not uncommon to find two pubs next door to each other. In Barrack Road, between Nelson Street and Leicester Street, was the *Britannia*, one of two pubs with that name in the borough, and adjoining it was the *Duke of Cambridge*. Both were demolished in 1932 and rebuilt in the modern style bearing the single name *'Britannia'*.

106 *(Above)* Though not adjoining, the *Phoenix Tavern*, originally known as Adam's beerhouse, and the *Midland Tavern*, also originally a beerhouse cum grocer's shop, could hardly have been closer, facing each other across the very narrow Swan Street. The *Phoenix* survived until 1940, while the Midland lasted into the mid-1950s.

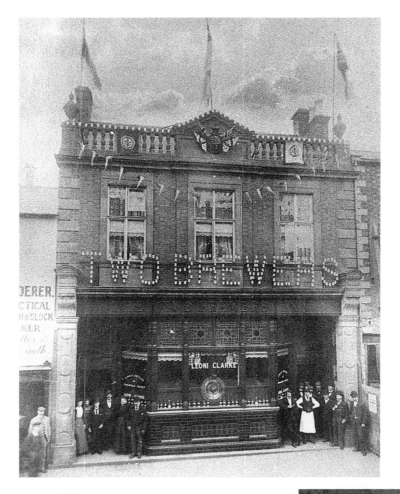

107 The *Two Brewers* was in Abington Street, a few doors westward of Wood Street. The once pokey little pub was rebuilt in the London style, all mahogany and brass, and the licence taken by Mr. Leoni Clarke. He was an ex-Music Hall artiste who billed himself as the Cat King, presenting a troupe of performing cats! He then went on to tour with a mixed group that included pigs, goats and ducks, before graduating to a boxing kangaroo! When the kangaroo died he retired from the boards and took over the *Two Brewers*, turning it into a haven for visiting variety artistes.

108 As for the kangaroo ... he had it stuffed and mounted over the bar!

109 The *Bantam Cock*, on Abington Square, has a long history dating back to 1486. In days gone by when the public gallows was at the Racecourse, this was the last stop for condemned criminals who were allowed to pause and spend their cash. Locals, knowing this, would congregate here anticipating free drinks. As seen here, it was the last surviving thatched house in the borough. This century it has been rebuilt in the mock-Tudor style and subsequently gutted to redecorate in a mock-Victorian style!

110 Pub outings were popular, an annual fixture being the nutting party like this preparing to set off from the *Red House*, now the *Red Rover*, on the Weedon Road. A number of horse brakes loaded with men and beer-barrels would go into the countryside to collect chestnuts, cobnuts and beechnuts ... at least, that was the idea!

111 The most popular pub game, locally, was quoits, the national body of which, the Shakespeare Quoits Club, had its headquarters and its renowned quoits court at the *Black Lion* in St Giles's Street. One of the best teams in these parts was that of the *Queen Adelaide* pub in Kingsthorpe village, who pose for the camera here.

CHARACTERS

112 Every town had its characters and Northampton was no different. Old Poppitt was employed by the corporation as a roadman and water carrier. He had extremely bowed legs between which he would carry a watering can suspended from a neck-strap. With this he sprinkled the dirt roads to keep down the dust in summer. Facially he resembled the Duke of Wellington, a resemblance increased by his habitual dress of corduroy breeches, buckskin waistcoat, old-fashioned swallowtail coat, and stove-pipe beaver hat. He lived in a makeshift shelter in the grounds of Vigo Gardens (where the hospital now stands).

113 Among the many street piano players one notable local character was Blind Bellamy with his boy Joe.

114 An extraordinary man was Joe Ingram, a native of Harrowden. He was frequently seen in Northampton, though, as he was a steeplejack and a champion pedestrian. As he maintained most of the local factory chimneys and church spires he experimented with parachutes, earning himself the nickname 'Parachute Joe'. He also designed and flew model aeroplanes, making so many strange predictions of what aeroplanes would one day be capable of that he was pilloried in the local press and thought to be insane. He foretold mass bombing, aerial invasion, and predicted that planes would eventually be capable of carrying a hundred or more people!

115 Solicitor and sports enthusiast Pat Darnell wore the Victorian garb of silk-faced frock coat, wing collar, silk cravat and top hat throughout his life. Although known throughout the county as 'Pat' Darnell, his given names were Albert Joseph, and he was born in the town on Valentine's Day 1865. He played cricket for Northamptonshire, served for many years as the honorary secretary of the Northamptonshire County Cricket Club, as well as serving on the M.C.C. Advisory Council. He became the first president of the Cobblers in 1897 and led the club into prominence and popularity. He went on to become one of the legislators of the council of the Football Association, president of both the Southern Football league and the Northampton Football Association. He was a great supporter, too, of the Saints rugby football team, as well as being borough coroner. In January 1955 he was taken ill, eventually dying nearly three months later, at the age of 91. With his passing went one of the last of the Northampton characters, a genuine Victorian gentleman.

THE FIRST WORLD WAR

116 The Welsh Fusiliers arrive in town in 1915, marching up the Wellingborough road.

117 Artillery was based at a camp established on the Racecourse. Gunners ride their limbers up Black Lion Hill on their way from the railway station, watched by two young women.

118 Eager to emulate their older 'brothers-in-arms', the urchins of the East Street gang, just off the Wellingborough Road, learnt to march and to drill, carved themselves wooden rifles, bought odd items of surplus army uniform, and called themselves the East End Bantam Fusiliers. They gave demonstrations of drill in streets and suburbs, collecting money and produce for wounded soldiers convalescing in local hospitals. Here they pose proudly for their 'regimental photograph'.

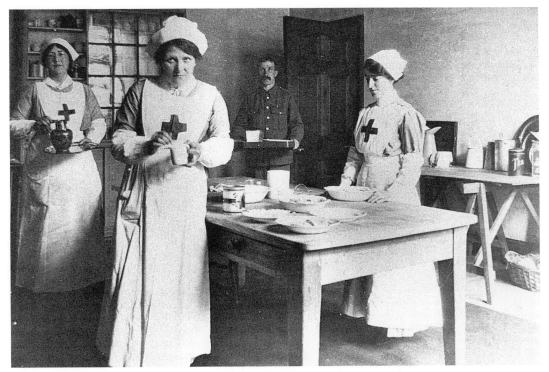

119 What had formerly been Berrywood Lunatic Asylum became the Duston War Hospital, housing many wounded and shell-shocked servicemen. As well as regular staff, there were Medical Corps personnel, nurses from the women's service arms and many local voluntary organisations serving there. In this photograph nurses of the Red Cross prepare food in the kitchens at Berrywood.

120 On the Market Square a captured German Fokker monoplane is exhibited in connection with a fund-raising campaign.

121 The first cenotaph in Northampton was a temporary construction erected on the pavement in Abington Street especially for Heroes Day, 7 September 1919. On that day 8,000 local ex-servicemen marched past the memorial.

122 Edgar Mobbs, captain of the Saints rugby football team and holder of seven England caps, recruited his own sportsmen's battalion when the First World War broke out. He was killed in 1917 and a memorial to him and his fallen comrades was erected on the Market Square after the war. In later years the memorial was deemed to be a traffic hazard and was removed to the new Garden of Rest at Abington Square in 1937.

LEISURE AND PLEASURE

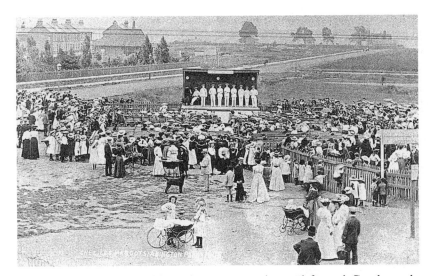

123 Bert Grapho and Billy Jackson got together and formed Grapho and Jackson's Pierrots in 1905, performing on some waste ground just outside Abington Park, on the Wellingborough road. The Pierrots gradually evolved into a concert party, the Chez Les Mascots, as seen here in a view taken from the *Abington Park Hotel* in 1906.

124 By 1911 Bert Grapho had developed his troupe and renamed it the Jovial Jollies.

125 On the same site, starting on Easter Monday 1905, a company called Miniature Railways of Great Britain Ltd., headed by local model engineer Bassett-Lowke, set up a model railway.

126 A hand-turned children's roundabout, the Mountain Pony Circus, is set up as part of a fair held on the Market Square some time in the 1890s.

127 The uniform of the Boy Scouts, based as it was on the military uniform of the Boer War campaign, looks rather quaint to today's eyes, but was very distinctive. This group of boys are from the Christchurch troop. The Boy Scouts were formed by Lt. Gen. Sir Robert S.S. Baden-Powell in 1908.

128 An older organisation, originally formed to give military training to boys from 12 to 18, was the Boys Brigade, a Northampton contingent of which is seen marching past the Manfield shoe factory on the Wellingborough road.

129 Every church had its regular bazaars. This event with a Japanese theme at the St Giles's Church rooms in the 1890s shows great ingenuity in its decoration.

130 The Cycle Parade started in 1890 and grew out of a fancy dress bicycle ride from Regent Square to Franklins Gardens called the Top Hat Run. Two entrants in a parade *c.*1900 await the judging on the Market Square. With snake skins around her neck, wrists and waist, the lady is advertising a brand of Turkish cigarette called Snake Charmer, sold in king-sized cork-tipped form at 3s. 2d. for twenty-five.

131 In 1930 a great Historical Pageant was held at Abington Park. Chain mail and halberds was the order of the day for these two 'soldiers' guarding the entrance to Abington Manor.

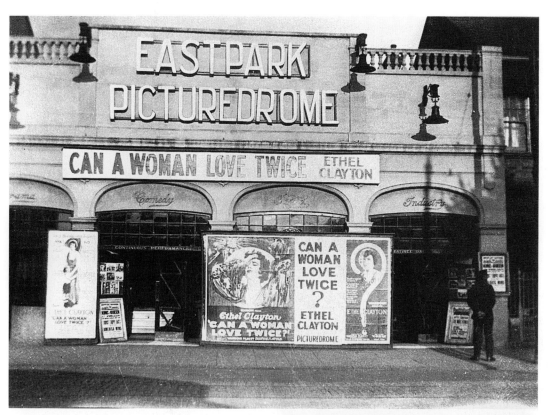

132 The East Park Picturedrome was a cinema built by Mr. Robinson, a stonemason by trade, on his yard on the Kettering road. When opened on 21 November 1912, the cinema was considered one of the most modern in the town. In 1930 a young Northampton artist, Henry Bird, then 21 years old, winner of a travelling art scholarship and sponsored by Northampton Rotary Club, decorated the walls of the auditorium with modern murals. In later life he achieved national fame.

133 Every cinema had its commissionaire, uniformed and formidable, directing clients to the correct queues or shouting 'Seats in all parts!', depending on how business was going. The guardian of the Picturedrome appears less daunting than most of his ilk.

134 Advertising the film 'Swing High', which was showing at the Temperance Hall in Newland, an elephant and a couple of educated ponies attract a curious crowd on the Market Square.

135 Innocent fun in the paddling pool at Abington Park in the 1930s. The Broadley-head Spring, which used to supply water to the manor in days gone by, was channelled through a series of three lakes, the upper one being concreted to form a boating and paddling pool.

CEREMONIES AND CELEBRATIONS

136 The stone-laying ceremony for the new Town Hall on 22 October 1861. The mayor Ald. Pickering Phipps prepares to address the crowd.

137 To celebrate the marriage of Prince Albert Edward, Prince of Wales, to Princess Alexandra of Denmark on 10 March 1863, ox-roasts took place in several areas of the town. In the pleasure gardens behind the *Green Man Inn* at St James's End an ox, a sheep, a pig and a hare were roasted, the spit being turned by an agricultural steam engine. The feast was presided over by the pub's landlord John Collier who bore most of the cost. The meat was distributed to every resident of St James's End, then merely a small hamlet.

138 In July of 1873 a new cattle market was opened on ground down by the river. Complaints about cattle being driven into the centre of town for the Market Square sales had escalated and forced the move. Opening day saw the site unfinished and the navvies' barrows still in the foreground.

139 A temporary wooden building was erected on the new cattle market site to house a great Leather Exhibition to launch the project. Two policemen guard the exhibits which arrived from all over the world, so many that an overflow display had to be arranged at the Town Hall. Nearly 50,000 people paid to visit the exhibition.

140 On Wednesday, 8 June 1904 the foundation stone of a new church was laid at Abington, to be called Christchurch. Two years later it was consecrated but, thanks to the intervention of two World Wars, the church was never completed. To this day it is lacking the fine tower that architect Matthew Holding designed for it.

141 Great excitement followed Queen Victoria's Diamond Jubilee in 1897. It is early morning on 22 June and residents of St James's End walk to town along Marefair for the celebrations. Above the distant buildings can be seen the six-foot-high metal top hat that advertised Partridge's men's-wear shop. On the right the old *Rose and Punchbowl* inn was being rebuilt as the *Rose and Punchbowl Hotel*.

142 The town was well decorated. Abington Street, a narrow funnel as seen from the Market Square, was a mass of flags.

143 The Market Square itself, viewed here from Wood Hill, was thronged.

144 Elsewhere separate celebrations were going on. On Regent Square crowds were gathering. The fountain in the foreground was erected in 1860 in honour of the Rev. Thomas Hutton, chaplain of the nearby prison for 11 years, for his efforts in upholding temperance and education. The edifice was demolished in December 1953 when a car crashed into it. It was never re-erected.

145 On the Racecourse a crowd of nearly 20,000 children assembled from schools throughout the area. Over 25,000 adults also gathered to celebrate with patriotic songs, demonstrations by local organisations and speeches. The grandstand, nowadays the Pavilion Restaurant, was packed.

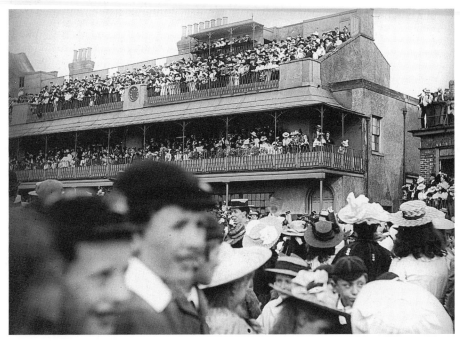

146 In 1900 it was proposed to hold the Northamptonshire Agricultural Society's County Show on the Racecourse and for it to be opened by the Duke of York. Some local folk felt it to be inappropriate with many men away in South Africa fighting the Boer War. However, the show went ahead and the town was decorated throughout for the occasion. Here, in the flag-bedecked Drapery, a horse tram bound for Kingsthorpe passes beneath a 'venetian arch'.

147 On 20 September 1913 the mayor, Councillor Harvey Reeves, declared open the Edward VII memorial outside General Hospital on the corner of Billing Road and Cheyne Walk. The £1,200 cost was raised by public subscription. Designed by Sir George Frampton, it features a portrait bust of the king and above it the figure of St George killing the dragon of disease.

148 Three days later, on 23 September 1913, King George and Queen Mary visited the town and received a civic welcome on the Market Square. The king and queen were staying with the Spencers at Althorp whilst attending the vast army manoeuvres that took place throughout the Midlands.

149 After inspecting the guard of honour, the king met veterans of the Crimean War and the Indian Mutiny. Among them he was surprised to meet Colonel Campbell of Salcey Lawn who had been his aide-de-camp when, as Prince of Wales, he had toured India. The elderly lady was Mrs. Mason, widow of one of the 'Noble Six Hundred' at the Charge of the Light Brigade.

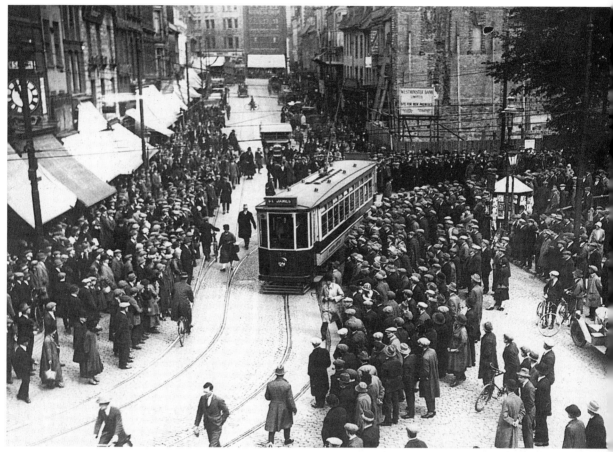

150 The General Strike of May 1926 passed fairly quietly in Northampton except when Mr. Cameron, the tramway manager, decided to run a passenger tram through the town centre. Strikers had allowed repair work to proceed during the conflict and maintenance vehicles to continue running, but this was too much. A hostile crowd waylaid the tram and stormed it, intent on evicting the passengers. Violent scuffles ensued and police drew truncheons to mount a baton charge. Several arrests were made.

151 The Prince of Wales visited the town on the seventh day of the seventh month of 1927, thought then to be a good omen. Mistakenly, as it turned out, for as King Edward VIII he reigned only briefly, abdicating in the wake of the Mrs. Simpson row. Among the places that he visited was Sears' shoe factory. To the right of the prince is the mayor, Councillor James Peach.

152 In August 1930 the Australian test cricket team came to Northampton to play the county side. Some of the players, led by the legendary Don Bradman, found time to cheer up young patients at Manfield Orthopaedic Hospital, who had formed their own boy scout troop.

153 When the Duke of York came to the town in May 1930 little did he realise that he would become King George VI upon his brother's abdication. It was Northampton Festival Week, with trade exhibitions and an historical pageant at Abington Park. Visiting the General Hospital to lay the foundation stone of a new ophthalmic ward, the duke was accompanied by the mayor, Councillor Ralph Smith and Sir Charles Knightley as he passed through a welcoming parade of V.A.D. nurses.

154 *(Top right)* Crowds stand in silence outside All Saints' Church on 28 January 1936 to honour the late King George V. A memorial service was being held inside.

155 *(Bottom right)* On the Market Square Evangeline Booth of the Salvation Army addresses a large congregation of supporters. When William Booth, the founder of the movement, first visited the town in 1882 he was stoned by townsmen, tar was tipped into his carriage, and the instruments of his band were smashed. He received a warmer welcome when he returned in 1905.

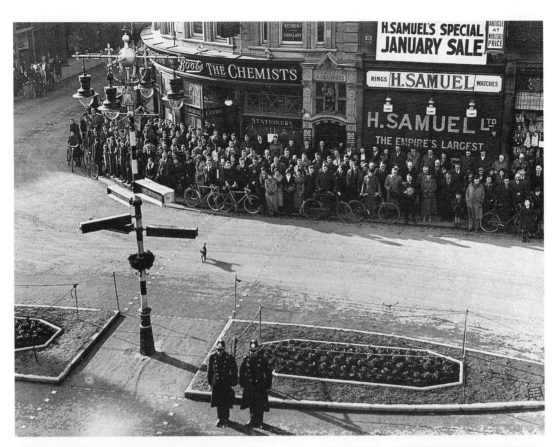

156 The Coronation of George VI on 12 May 1937 was joyfully celebrated after the turmoil of the Edward VIII and Mrs. Simpson affair. The Drapery was en fête for the occasion.

157 The civic procession passes along Mercers' Row to a service on the Market Square on Coronation Day 1937. The parade included a contingent of nurses from the hospital.

158 Each year on Oak Apple Day, 29 May, tradition demands that an oak leaf garland is placed around the statue of King Charles II above the portico of All Saints' Church. This is in gratitude for the gift of 1,000 tons of timber from the nearby royal forests for the rebuilding of the church after the Great Fire of Northampton in 1675.

159 Another, more recent, annual ceremony was the service to mark Anzac Day, seen here at Towcester Road cemetery, where fallen servicemen from Australia and New Zealand are buried.

160 In July 1946 the young Princess Elizabeth, stunning in a periwinkle-blue dress, visited the district. At the General Hospital she was accompanied by Earl Spencer as she passed through a guard of honour of nursing staff.

161 At the nearby Barratt Maternity Home her guard of honour was of local A.T.S. girls. The princess had served with this force during the war.

162 During her visit she also inspected a flight of the Air Training Corps.

163 February 1952 saw the accession of Elizabeth II. The proclamation was made from the steps of the fountain on the Market Square by the mayor, Councillor Frank Lee.

164 The celebrations for the Coronation that occurred the following June were a welcome break from post-war austerity. The cramped cul-de-sac of Gladstone Terrace had never needed much excuse for a knees-up and excelled itself with a canopy of flags and bunting.

165 In Orchard Street in St James's End local children admire the patriotic display devised by Mr. George Rich in a garage entrance.

166 Children of Stimpson Avenue School line up to collect their Coronation souvenirs.

167 In College Street traders put on their own tableaux. Queen Elizabeth I (Miss Freda Spatcher) knights Sir Walter Raleigh (Mr. G.M. Hall) as part of the Coronation celebrations.

168 St Katharine's Church, in King Street, was built in 1839 as an overflow facility for All Saints'. When it was demolished in 1950 the area was partly given over to a small memorial garden. It was planned to feature a sculpture by Professor Frank Dobson called *Woman with Fish*. Here firemen fill the surrounding pool, while the statue remains swathed in tarpaulin.

169 May 1952 and Sir Frank Dobson unveils his statue while the mayor, Alderman Frank Lee, gives it a dubious glance. The statue was intended to spout water from the fish's mouth, but vandalism soon prevented that. The figure suffered many indignities, having bras and other sundry items placed on it. When hooligans finally broke off its head the statue was removed and, after a time, re-erected in Delapre Park Gardens.

THE SECOND WORLD WAR

170 With war looming the authorities prepared for the expected onslaught by digging trenches and shelters on the Racecourse.

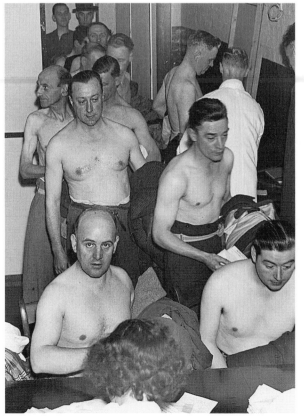

171 *(Above)* In 1938 National Defence became Air Raid Precautions in readiness for attack. Here a policeman, right, checks the gas masks and equipment of an A.R.P. rescue squad. The men wore oilskins in expectation of gas attack. On the helmets 'R' indicates Rescue personnel, 'D.C.' Decontamination.

172 *(Left)* Although conscription was confined to the younger age groups at first, older men rushed to volunteer for the auxiliary services. At the Drill Hall recruits undergo medical examination.

173 *(Top right)* The Local Defence Volunteers were formed in May 1940, the month that Winston Churchill formed a coalition government following the resignation of Neville Chamberlain. Jokers quipped that 'LDV' stood for 'Look, Duck and Vanish'. Churchill, sensibly, changed the name to Home Guard on 23 July. This group is of railway employees who formed the Northampton L.M.S. Railway group of the L.D.V. Drilling the men is ex-Regimental Sergeant Major G. Quartermain, holder of the D.C.M. and the Military Medal.

174 *(Bottom right)* Food rationing brought shortages and the scarcity of unrationed produce created unprecedented queues like this one on the Market Square.

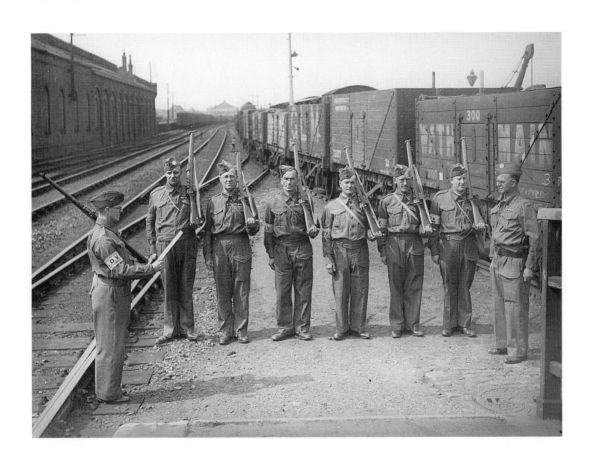

175 (*Above*) Many fund-raising events on the Market Square were held to encourage donations for the purchase of arms. Salute the Soldier Week, in June 1943, saw a display of tanks overwhelmed by an 'army' of urchins.

176 (*Left*) With entertainment limited, many children attended the Saturday morning cinema clubs. Tommy Handley, the most popular radio comic of the day and star of the hit programme, 'It's That Man Again', or ITMA, leads members of the Gaumont British Club at the Exchange Cinema in the club song during a visit in 1944.

177 (*Right*) After the euphoria of VE and VJ days, a quieter Thanksgiving Day was held in October 1945. Preparations, erecting a dais and bringing in a Spitfire and armoured cars, had to be accomplished amid the hustle and bustle of a normal market day.

178 As servicemen returned home they all arrived to a warm welcome, but none as spirited as that which Corporal Alan Norman received at Gladstone Terrace. He had spent a long period in a German prisoner-of-war camp. Despite there being only 74 small houses in the Terrace, it sent 124 men into the forces during the war, of whom 24 died.

179 Upon the return of the Northamptonshire Regiment from the Far East, the town conferred the Freedom of the Borough upon it on Victory Day, 8 June 1946. The colour party present arms for the first time with bayonets fixed, one of the privileges allowed by the Freedom. Others marched through the town with flags flying and bands played without seeking permission.

Index

Roman numerals refer to pages in the introduction and arabic numerals to individual illustrations.